fao economic and social development paper

18

D1299877

china: agriculture in transition

report of fao mission on
agricultural planning and policy
28 july-12 august 1980

FOOD AND AGRICULTURE ORGANIZATION OF THE UNITED NATIONS
Rome 1981

The designations employed and the presentation
of material in this publication do not imply the
expression of any opinion whatsoever on the
part of the Food and Agriculture Organization
of the United Nations concerning the legal
status of any country, territory, city or area or
of its authorities, or concerning the delimitation
of its frontiers or boundaries.

M-00

ISBN 92-5-101068-4

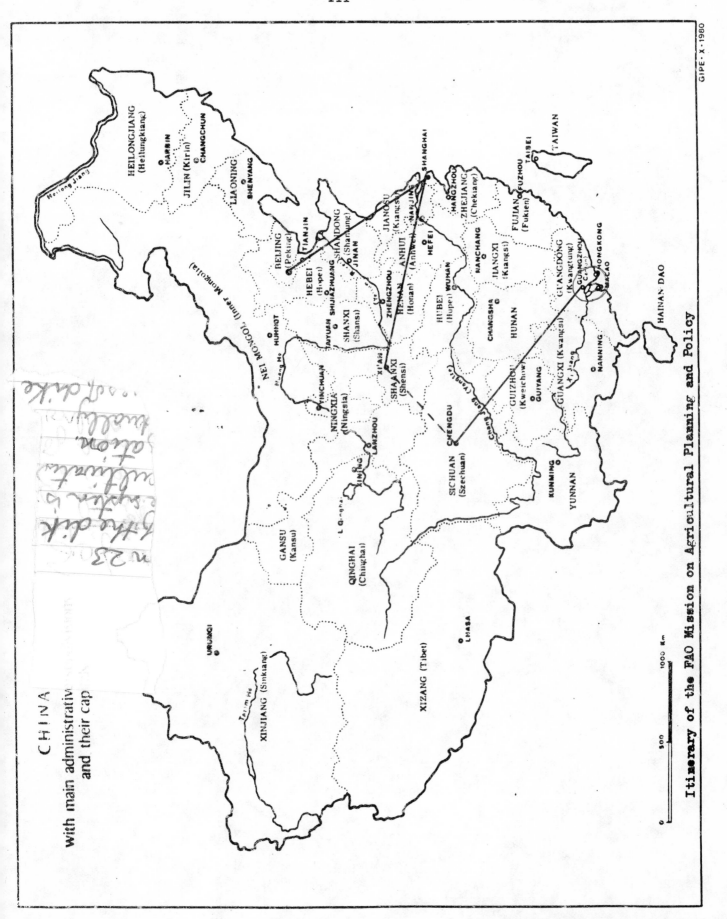

Itinerary of the FAO Mission on Agricultural Planning and Policy

TABLE OF CONTENTS

Page

PREFACE ..... vii-viii

I. CHINESE ECONOMY: SOME BASIC FACTS 1

II. AGRICULTURAL STRUCTURE AND PLANNING 3
   A. Political and agricultural structure 3
   B. Agricultural planning 4
      1. Planning experience 4
      2. Principles, objectives and procedures of planning 7
   C. Measures undertaken since 1977 for improving planning 9
   D. Major issues in planning 13
      1. Development strategy 13
         i) Land expansion 13
         ii) Intensification 14
         iii) Irrigation 14
      2. Yield potential 15
      3. Livestock development 16
      4. Mechanization and employment 16
      5. Import of grain 16
      6. Investment allocation 17
      7. Financing 17
      8. Income distribution 18

III. AGRICULTURAL POLICIES AND INCENTIVES 19
   A. Agricultural policies, incentives and related institutions 19
      1. Agricultural prices 19
      2. Agricultural taxes 21
      3. Consumption subsidies 21
      4. Agricultural credit 22
      5. Purchase and supply cooperatives 22
      6. Other incentives 23

7.	Sideline enterprises	23
8.	Workpoint system	24
B.	Major issues concerning agricultural policies and incentives	30
1.	Production pattern adjustments	30
2.	Price adjustments	30
3.	Allocative efficiency of resources	31
4.	Subsidies	31
5.	Investment funds	31
6.	Role of markets	32
7.	Manpower utilization	33
8.	Income inequalities	33
IV.	AGRICULTURAL EDUCATION, TRAINING AND RESEARCH	35
A.	Existing structure	35
B.	Major issues	38
1.	Agricultural education	38
2.	Training	38
3.	Research	38
Appendix 1 – Main Locations Visited and Principal Officials and People Met		39
Bibliography		43

PREFACE

At the invitation of the Government of the People's Republic of China, I visited China from 28 July to 12 August 1980. I was accompanied by Mr. K.A.P. Stevenson, Chief, Agricultural Education and Extension Service, Human Resources, Institutions and Agrarian Reform Division, Dr. N.S. Randhawa, Senior Economist, Planning Assistance Service, Policy Analysis Division, and Mr. H.J. Scheidt, Associate Expert in the Office of the Assistant Director-General, Economic and Social Policy Department.

The purpose of our visit was to familiarize ourselves with the recent changes in the Chinese agricultural policies and developments, including procedures and techniques of planning, as well as production, consumption, distribution and investment policies. It was also expected that the visit would afford an opportunity to have some idea about the future perspectives of the Chinese food and agricultural sector.

The itinerary included visits to Beijing, Shanghai, Xi'an, Chengdu and Guangzhou, where discussions were held at all levels, National Government, State Government, Department, County and Commune. The Communes visited varied in scope and purpose and presented an overview of the different aspects of Chinese agriculture and agro-industry. Within the communes, discussions were also held at the levels of brigades and production teams.

We express our deep appreciation to the Government of the People's Republic of China for the very considerable efforts they made to make the trip extremely rewarding. Special thanks are due to Mr. Hao Zhongsi, Vice Minister of Agriculture, Beijing, and Mr. Yang Zhong, Deputy Governor of Sichuan province, who received the group and gave us the benefit of their considerable experience. We were accompanied throughout by Mr. Wu Tian-Xi, Deputy Chief Engineer and Mr. Zhang Jianhai, Interpreter. Mr. Wu's wide knowledge of the communes was of great value to us in deepening our understanding of the Chinese agriculture. We are grateful to Mr. Zhang for his indefatigable efforts in interpretation throughout our visit.

At first, we did not think of writing a report since this visit
was neither a study tour nor a technical mission. However, in view of
the great interest shown by our hosts and pains taken by them to inform,
explain and participate in long and detailed discussions with us on
various aspects of the Chinese agricultural policies, we thought it
might be useful to record our views and observations, for whatever they
are worth, at least for clarifying our own thoughts, if nothing else.

Dr. N. S. Randhawa contributed considerably to the preparation of
this report incorporating the views and impressions of all of us. The
report has, of course, benefited not only from the comments of our
Chinese hosts, but also from senior officers in FAO.

Nurul Islam
Assistant Director-General
Economic and Social Policy Department

I. CHINESE ECONOMY: SOME BASIC FACTS

China has a total geographical area of 960 million hectares, of which about 100 to 107 million hectares, forming only about 11 percent, are arable. The total population was estimated at 970.9 million in 1979, and it formed about one-fourth of the world population. The annual growth rate of population in 1979 was reported as 1.1 percent. The rural population was estimated at about 800 million, comprising as much as 82 percent of the total population. Out of the total labour force of 450 million, about 310 million, constituting about 70 percent, were engaged in agriculture.

The total gross output from industry and agriculture was 617.5 billion yuan [1] in 1979. Agriculture contributed only 26 percent (158.4 billion yuan) of the gross output with 70 percent of the total labour. In 1979, the annual growth rate of gross output was 8.5 percent over 1978, and the rates of growth for industry and agriculture were 8.5 and 8.6 percent respectively. Faster rates were achieved in some sub-sectors: grain 9 percent, oil bearing crops 23 percent, beetroot 15 percent, silk cocoons 19 percent, and livestock products 24 percent. The output of grain per (cultivated) hectare was 4.1 tons, per agricultural worker 1,100 kg., and per capita of total population 342 kg. Overall food grains consumption per capita was 240 kg. in rural areas and 180 kg. in urban areas.

Agricultural development has been given high priority in recent years. The proportion of total investment for agriculture was increased from 10.4 percent in 1978 to 14 percent in 1979, and is likely to be raised further to 18 percent by 1985.

The crop sector is still predominant. It contributed about 60 percent to the total agricultural output in 1979, as against livestock 14 percent, forestry 3 percent, fisheries 1.5 percent and sideline

---

[1] 1 yuan = U.S. $0.62

enterprises including industrial enterprises in communes 21.5 percent. The distribution of agricultural gross output among major components in 1979 was as follows:

Item	Percent
Production & management cost	33.6
Tax	3.2
Collective reserves	9.6
Sub-total	46.4
Individual share for distribution to members	53.6
Total	100.0

The breakdown of the collective reserves was as follows: accumulation fund 5.2 percent, grain reserve fund 0.7 percent, welfare fund 1.8 percent, and production cost fund (depreciation, etc.) 1.9 percent.

II. AGRICULTURAL STRUCTURE AND PLANNING

A. Political and agricultural structure

China has no head of state. This function is performed by the Chairman of the Standing Committee of the National People's Congress (NPC) which is the "highest organ of state power". It has at present more than 3,000 deputies. The Standing Committee is the permanent organ of the NPC, and the State Council is the executive arm of the State. The Chinese Communist Party (CCP) has its parallel authority with the Central Committee and the politburo of the Central Committee.

At the lower levels, there are local people's congresses and their Standing Committees known as the Revolution Committees, which were introduced during the Cultural Revolution and have recently been restricted to provincial and municipal levels.

The State Planning Commission under the State Council is responsible for coordinating the planning work of all the sectors and for formulating overall plans. The planning work is integrated at the provincial level. The National People's Congress is the final authority for approving economic plans and State budgets submitted by the State Council.

The State Agricultural Commission, a high-ranking body under the State Council, was established in February 1979 to draw up agricultural plans in cooperation with the State Planning Commission, to coordinate the functions and to monitor the performance of the Ministries of Agriculture, Forestry, Agricultural Machinery, Water Conservancy, State Farms and Land Reclamation, and Food. Among the coordinating and monitoring functions of the Commission, the major ones are: agricultural resources and their utilisation, planning, education, policies and legal aspects. The Commission also makes its own field investigations to assist it in performing its functions.

The Chairman of the State Agricultural Commission is a Vice-Premier, and there are five Vice-Chairmen. Membership includes the ministers from the above six ministries and also ministers from other agricultural-related ministries.

It is not intended to state the functions of each of the above ministries in detail. However, for example, the major functions of the **Ministry of Agriculture** include production planning, management of commune enterprises, arrangements for supplies of inputs, implementation of agricultural policies, monitoring and evaluation of plans and programmes, studies and investigations, agricultural education, science and technology, and proposals for planning and policies. At the provincial level the Ministry provides technical guidance to the staff engaged in agricultural activities, but the administrative control of the staff lies with the provincial governments.

Administratively, the country is divided into 29 units, 21 provinces excluding Taiwan, 5 autonomous regions and 3 municipalities. The agrarian structure consists of 53,000 people's communes (average population 14,500 per commune, average cultivated area of 1,945 ha.). The communes are further sub-divided into 698,000 brigades (about 13 brigades per commune with an average population of 1,100 and an average cultivated area of 148 ha.) and 5,150,000 production teams (about 7 production teams per brigade with an average population of 150 and an average cultivated area of 20 hectares). In addition there are some suburban communes located near large urban centres and about 2,048 state farms located in northeast, northwest and south China having cultivated areas of about 4 million hectares (average size about 2,000 ha.), about 4 percent of the total cultivated areas of the country.

B.   Agricultural planning
1.   Planning experience
The People's Republic of China was founded on 1 October 1949. The period 1950-52 was mainly devoted to restoration and land reforms. This period was followed by the First Five-Year Plan, 1953-57, during which the basic structure for collectivization of agriculture was laid by establishing mutual aid teams (1952-56) which were transformed into agricultural producers' co-operatives (APC) and later into advanced agricultural producers' co-operatives (1957). Land reform, which led to distribution of about 50 million ha. of land to the peasants, and establishment of the co-operative agrarian structure were the main factors which led to significant agricultural development during the First Five-Year Plan period.

Encouraged by the achievements of the First Plan, in 1958 it was decided to accelerate the Second Five-Year Plan into "The Great Leap Forward". The socialistic transformation was taken a step further by establishing communes and linking them with brigades and production teams. But during 1959-61 floods, droughts and typhoons devastated the country, consequently the pace of agricultural development was seriously hampered, disincentives to peasants arising from the extremes to which some Great Leap policies were pushed, further adversely affected the agricultural growth, and the Second Five-Year Plan was abandoned in 1960. Also the Soviet technicians were withdrawn in 1960.

Shocked by the damage done by natural hazards (1959-61), the Government considered it advisable to devote the following four years (1962-65) to readjustment and recovery and to gain further experience for agricultural development. The Third Five-Year Plan (1966-70) was launched in 1966 and the grain output surpassed in 1966 the peak level of 1958. The launching of the Cultural Revolution coincided with the starting of the Third Five-Year Plan and it continued till the end of the Fourth Plan (1971-75). The political turbulence caused during this period hampered greatly the pace of agricultural development, particularly in the initial periods of the Cultural Revolution (1966-69). The Fifth Five-Year Plan was due to start in 1976 but it was superseded by the comprehensive Ten-Year Economic Development Plan (1976-85), which emphasised modernization of four sectors - agriculture, industry, national defense, and science and technology. The value of gross agricultural output was estimated to increase at an annual rate of 4 to 5 percent. The Ten Year Plan's coup de grâce came in March 1979, one year after ratification by the Fifth National People's Congress on March 5, 1978, and a three-year period 1979-81 was designed to "readjust, restructure, consolidate and improve the national economy". During this transition period annual plans are being formulated and implemented.

Ex-Chairman Hua Guofeng stressed, at the Third Session of the Fifth National People's Congress held in August-September 1980, that some of the targets for the Ten-Year Plan were too high and declared that now

China was drafting a new Ten-Year Economic Plan (1981-90) and a Five-Year Plan (1981-85) would also be formulated.

Non-availability and inadequacy of data do not permit a precise estimation of the performance of the agricultural sector. However, according to an IFPRI study [1], the gross value of agricultural output (GVAO) increased at an annual rate of 2.9 percent during 1952-77, and the value added by agriculture, gross of depreciation charges on farm machinery, equipment, and service buildings, at 1.7 percent per annum. Since inputs rose during this period by 131 percent as against 97 percent increase in GVAO, the total factor productivity declined at an average rate of 0.65 percent per annum. The grain production rose by 2.3 percent per annum and it barely exceeded the 2.1 growth rate for population growth. In fact, the production of food grains per capita in 1978 was the same as in 1957.

The real domestic product may be said to have roughly increased at the rate of 5 percent per annum during this period. Taking an income elasticity for all food as 0.8 percent and population growth rate as 2.0 percent, the demand for food would have increased by 4.4 percent per annum; but food output increased a little more than population growth. Therefore the basic food balance was kept primarily by policies to restrict household incomes and rationing.

Considering natural hazards, socio-political upheavals, the momentous task of restoration and reconstruction of the economy, building of socialistic structures, and an explosive growth of population by more than 400 million which the country has faced since the liberation, the performance of the agricultural sector by no means is discouraging, in fact it is praiseworthy. The most spectacular achievement was the significant decrease in income inequalities brought about by land reforms and collectivization of economy. A sound socialistic agrarian structure

---

[1] Tang, Anthony M. and Stone, Bruce: Food Production in the People's Republic of China, Research Report 15. International Food Policy Research Institute, Washington, D. C. May 1980, 177 pp.

has already been established and with the necessary improvements and adjustments in the future, would make it possible to accelerate the rate of agricultural development significantly. The growth rate already achieved for gross value of agricultural output, was as much as 8.6 percent in 1979 over 1978 and 8.9 percent in 1978 over 1977.

2. Principles, objectives and procedures of planning

Agriculture as the foundation; industry as the leading sector; self-reliance; and "walking on two legs" have been the major guiding principles in planning and formulation of policies in the past. Though these principles are still maintained, modernization of agriculture, industry, national defense and science and technology has recently been emphasised, and particularly for the agricultural sector, integration of agriculture, industry and commerce is being given very high priority. Modernization of agriculture by the year 2000 is frequently declared as a long-run major objective.

Ex-Chairman Hua Guofeng, in his speech delivered at the 2nd Session of the Fifth National People's Congress, held on 18 June 1979, stated the following ten guidelines for the development of the economy:

- Uphold the guiding idea of taking agriculture as the foundation of our economy and concentrate effort on raising agricultural production;

- adopt resolute and effective measures to speed up the growth of light and textile industries;

- effectively overcome the weak links in the economy; the coal, petroleum and power industries, transport and communications services, and building material industry;

- resolutely curtail capital construction and try to get the best results from investment;

- vigorously develop science, education and culture and speed up the training of personnel for construction;

- continue to do a good job in importing technology, make active use of funds from abroad and strive to expand exports;

- adopt a resolute attitude and take active and steady steps to reform the structure of economic management;

- preserve basic price stability; readjust those prices that
  are irrational, while strengthening price control;

- raise the living standard of the people step by step as production rises; and

- continue to do a good job of family planning and effectively
  control population growth.

The procedures of planning are based on the major declaration such
as "from the top down, and from the bottom up"; and "leaving leeway",
which means allowing room for adjustments as production goes on. The
major procedure, "from the top down, and from the bottom up", didn't
function during the period of the Cultural Revolution as usually directives were given from the above to be implemented by the communes,
brigades and production teams. The normative appeals and coercive
measures used during this period greatly hampered the local initiative
and consequently adversely affected the pace of development. Now intensive efforts are being made to implement the above procedure in let-
ter and spirit in order to restore the confidence of local managements
in this procedure. Major steps taken towards this are: 1) the ownership of the people's communes, production brigades and production teams
and their power of self-management are to be protected by State laws;
2) the requisition or use of labour, land, draught animals, machinery,
funds, products and other materials of the production teams without com-
pensation is not allowed; 3) investigations are being made on land,
materials etc., taken from the production teams during the Cultural
Revolution so that these could be returned to them; 4) propaganda work
is being carried out among the masses for making members familiar with
their rights and the policies in order to bring into full play the role
of local management.

As mentioned earlier, the decision to formulate a new Ten-Year
Plan (1981-90) and a Five-Year Plan (1981-85) has recently been taken.
The State intends to apply thoroughly the above-mentioned procedure in
the formulation of these plans. In the meantime, the country has already
made significant progress in the application of this procedure in the
formulation and implementation of annual plans since 1976. In brief,

the State Planning Commission, on the suggestions and discussions with
the ministries concerned with agriculture and the State Agricultural
Commission, draws a tentative Annual Development Plan. Each tentative
provincial plan is forwarded to the province, which, in turn, transmits
it to the county through the district. Each county then calls a meeting
of commune leaders under them to discuss the commune plans. At this
stage the participation of the masses in planning starts. Then each commune holds a meeting of leaders of brigades and production teams under
them to examine the tentative State proposals for plans of each brigade
and production team. The proposed plan for each team and brigade is
critically examined by their members and their comments and suggestions
are transmitted to the communes. These suggestions are examined by the
leaders of the production teams and brigades at a meeting held at the
commune level to formulate a revised plan for the commune, which is then
transmitted to the county where the commune plans are integrated and
later transmitted to the provinces through their respective districts.
The provincial-revised plans are sent upwards to the concerned ministries,
the State Agricultural Commission and the Planning Commission. On the
basis of the suggestions from below, the State Planning Commission, in
consultation with the ministries concerned and the State Agricultural
Commission, formulates a revised plan. The revised plan is again sent
downwards following the same steps and the suggestions of the production
teams and communes are again conveyed upwards by the same process. In
the second revision from below, the conflicts and differences are nar-
rowed down. The State Planning Commission then finalises the annual
plan in consultation with the concerned ministries and the State Agricultural Commission and directives are sent downwards for implementation
of this plan. In short, the annual plan is finalised by two downward
and two upward movements and the agrarian structure - communes, brigades
and production teams - is conducive to the participation of the masses
in formulation of plans and policies and their implementation.

C.   Measures undertaken since 1977 for improving planning
       The State, since 1977, has undertaken significant measures to pro-
vide flexibility in agricultural plans of production teams and to

encourage the expansion of agricultural and non-agricultural sideline
enterprises. Some important measures among them are:

1.   During the Cultural Revolution, grain production was considered
the "key link", and its production was given the highest priority.
Therefore, the production teams were obliged to increase grain production,
which led to significant substitution of non-grain crops by grain crops
in areas where the non-grain crops had a comparative advantage. Consequently, the production of non-grain crops such as cotton and oil-
seeds suffered. Now with the active participation of production teams
in the planning process, their production plans are becoming more suitable to agro-ecological conditions. For instance, in the rural areas
adjacent to Shanghai, the area under cotton and rapeseed is being increased. Similarly in the northwestern part of Shaanxi province the
area under cotton which was reduced by 30 percent is now expanding.

2.   Previously, annual cropping patterns, production quotas and purchase quotas for each of the State-controlled commodities were given for
each production team and the team was directed to implement its plan.
Thus the production team practically could not make any changes in its
production plan. Now, generally production and purchase quotas for each
of these commodities are determined and purchase quotas are fixed for a
period of 5 years instead of every year, and teams are allowed to formulate cropping plans to meet these quotas. On a pilot scale, determination
of purchase quotas only, for providing more flexibility to the production
teams, is also being tried.

3.   Presently, the purchase quota for each controlled commodity is not
strictly applied. For example, a production team after meeting a mini-
mum level of purchase quota of rice, can meet its remaining purchase
quota by substituting other grains, namely wheat, soyabean, coarse grains
and potatoes and sweet potatoes. Similarly the purchase quota of other
grains mentioned above can be met by rice under certain conditions. The
substitution ratios between these grains have been fixed; for example,
one ton of soyabean is considered equivalent to two tons of other food

grains. In Cheng Chiao Commune in Sichuan province, the conversion ratios were more specifically reported as one ton of soyabean being equal to 1.2 tons of rice and the substitution ratio among wheat, rice and maize was on a 1:1 basis. In communes where per capita rice production is less than 260 kg. and coarse grains less than 210 kg., no purchase quota is fixed.

4. Some communes are being permitted to make their own production plans for some specified areas. For example, the Long March Commune near Shanghai City is permitted to formulate its own plan for 30 percent of its cultivated area on the condition that vegetables must be grown on this area, in addition to the production and purchase quotas for vegetables determined for the remaining 70 percent planned area. In another commune near Shanghai — Chengdong — though it was previously allowed in principle to formulate its own plan for 10 percent of its cultivated area, it was obliged to grow food grains on it, but now the commune can grow any kind of crop in this area.

5. Coordination between the production and consumption at commune level is being improved by considering the local taste and preferences in the formulation of the production plans. In the past, for instance, in the autonomous region of Tibet, the emphasis was placed on growing wheat, whereas the local population preferred barley; also in the country as a whole, maize production was over-emphasized considering its high yield and it replaced considerably wheat and soyabean which the communes preferred.

6. Private plots form a very small proportion of the cultivated area (about 7 percent) of the production teams. For each member the size of private plot is very small, about 0.008 ha. on the average, but it varies depending upon the availability and quality of land, and population pressure. For example, the average size of private plot is about 0.03 ha. in the Jin Ma Commune in the Sichuan province, 0.025 ha. in the China-Japan Friendship Commune near Beijing, and it is still smaller (0.01 ha.) in the Long March Commune in Shanghai province. Earlier the production

teams were coerced into growing food grains on their private plots also.
Now they are free to utilize their private plots in any way they like.
The areas under private plots have been increased in some communes. In
the Jin Ma Commune, the proportion of area under private plots has been
raised from 5 percent in 1976 to 10 percent in 1979.

7.   Previously leaders of communes, brigades and production teams were
usually nominated from above, but now they are elected by their respective
members. It has increased the participation of the members in formulation
of plans and their implementation.

8.   Attempts are being made to reduce the collective share (comprising
the reserve fund for investment and depreciation, welfare, etc.) in the
distribution of gross output of the production teams and to increase the
individual shares received by the members of the production teams. The
collective share in the Long March Commune near Shanghai has been decreased
from 14 percent in 1976 to 9 percent in 1979. The overall collective
share in the country is about 10 percent of the gross output, and it has
been reduced during the last two years. The decreasing of the collective
share has reduced the investment:income ratio, but has increased individual incomes.

Earlier, the production teams were allowed in principle but
were not permitted in practice to engage in sideline enterprises, and the
communes and brigades were also discouraged from undertaking sideline
enterprises. Now the establishment of sideline enterprises is being encouraged at all levels and the counties supply the list of possible enterprises which the communes can undertake. Significant progress in establishing sideline enterprises has been made during the last three to four
years and a substantial proportion of the income of production teams,
brigades and communes located near the towns and cities is now contributed by the agricultural and non-agricultural sideline enterprises; for
example, in the Ta Li Commune in Guangdong province, about 67 percent of
gross output was contributed by sideline enterprises.

10.   The members of the production teams are particularly encouraged to undertake agricultural sideline enterprises individually.

11.   Restrictions on selling the produce of State-controlled commodities in the free market have been relaxed; after meeting the purchase quotas, the excess quantities can be sold in the market. The communes, brigades and production teams can sell freely the non-controlled commodities in the free market, which previously was considered a social taboo.

12.   Great emphasis is being given to integrate agriculture, industry and commerce. On a pilot scale, joint enterprises for communes with Supply and Purchase Cooperatives have been established in the Sichuan province and a dominant role for communes is given in them. The communes act as a sub-company to the Supply and Purchase Cooperatives in these enterprises, thus a timely supply of required inputs is ensured, the disposal of produce is facilitated and as much as 90 percent of profits from these transactions go to the commune.

A number of significant changes have also been made in agricultural policies, to improve the internal terms of trade for the agricultural sector and provide incentive to communes, brigades, production teams and individual members to support the above-mentioned changes in planning and will be discussed in the following section. These changes in planning and policies must have contributed towards achieving higher rates of growth in 1978 and 1979 as compared to 1977.

D.   Major issues in planning
1.   Development strategy
        i) Land expansion
        Of the total land area of 960 million ha., only 105 million ha. - forming 11 percent of total land area - are arable, and per capita arable land is 0.11 ha. as compared to 0.25 ha. in India and 0.9 ha. in the USA. It is understood that the arable area can be extended by about 33 million ha. in the long run, of which 7 million ha. are of relatively better quality. These land expansion possibilities mostly exist in the north-east and northwest, and the cost of developing these lands appears high.

Also, these areas are sparsely populated. Therefore, in addition to investment, migration to these places will also be necessary.

ii) Intensification

Because of scarcity of land, China's agriculture has been characterised by intensive input of labour on a limited supply of land, steady expansion of multiple cropping, exacting crop rotations, improved irrigation, heavier doses of organic fertilizer and substantial increases in inorganic fertilizers. Though further intensification is possible, it would require much greater effort in the future than in the past. In fact, in Sichuan province, a reduction in the intensity of land use is advocated by replacing the one-year rotation of wheat/rice (summer)/rice (autumn), with wheat/rice (summer) because in the former rotation the yield of rice (autumn) is low due to low temperatures and there are labour constraints as well. The replacement of rice (autumn) where possible with maize or a maize and sweet potatoes mixture, is recommended by the Government.

iii) Irrigation

In China, irrigation is considered as the life blood of agriculture. At present, about 47 million ha., forming about 46 percent of the arable area, are irrigated. Substantial development of irrigation has taken place in the past. One of the most important irrigation potentials is provided by the Yangtse River, which has 20 times the flow of the Yellow River and could provide water to north China where it is most needed, but its development needs heavy investment. It is understood that the potential for irrigation development in the country is at present being studied.

China's agriculture is, therefore, faced with limited land expansion possibilities, intensification requiring comparatively more effort, and irrigation development demanding heavier investment. Therefore, an appropriate combination of land expansion, intensification and irrigation development needs to be formulated. For this purpose, studies on land use planning and regional development need to be conducted to guide the changes in production patterns towards attaining an optimal utilization of the existing cultivated area, to exploit rationally land expansion possibilities, and to bring about agricultural development in general. It hardly needs to be stressed that without development of adequate facilities for transporting surplus agricultural produce to locations where it is needed, the regional development of agriculture will be severely constrained.

Modernization and liberalization are the cornerstone of a new development strategy, and material incentives provided by the new economic policy will increase demand for consumer goods. Therefore, the supply of agricultural products should increase at a sufficient rate to meet the increasing demand, otherwise it will create problems of enormous proportion of unmet demand and cause inflation.

2.   Yield potential

China's overall yields are somewhat above the world average, and yet these are well below those in most of the developed countries. Thus there is admittedly a good potential for raising yields.

The mission visited only one research station, and based on the discussions at this station, and with the research staff working in communes visited by the mission (relatively progressive communes), it appeared that yields in trials and demonstration plots were not always much higher than in the fields of the production teams. It may be indicative of the fact that research for varieties of crops with higher potential yields has not been significantly advanced, and it may act as a serious constraint for increasing yields of crops in the medium term. It appears that agriculture research suffered badly during the Cultural Revolution and strenuous efforts will be needed to evolve varieties with a much higher yield potential as soon as possible.

At present, the use of fertilizers per ha. is estimated at about 89 kgs. of nutrient from chemical fertilizers and about 55 kgs. from organic fertilizers. It is one of the important reasons for high yields

in China. However, the use of chemical fertilizers is still well below
those of the developed countries with high yields. Therefore, it is
particularly important that the increase in supply of chemical fertilizers
be given high priority.

3.   Livestock development

China has huge tracts of grassland, close to 300 million ha.,
where livestock production is carried on. It is assumed that area under
pasture can be extended by 200 million ha. Thus there is a vast potential for the development of the livestock industry. Because of over-
emphasis on grain production during the Cultural Revolution, its production was extended to some marginal lands, including encroachment on
pastures, which resulted in reduction of livestock production. To meet
the demand for livestock products in the future and to improve nutri-
tional levels, the development of the livestock industry is very important.

4.   Mechanization and employment

Mechanization of agricultural operations, mainly preparatory
operations, has been completed on about 40 million ha., forming about
38 percent of the arable area. The agricultural operations are comparatively more mechanized in the northeast and north than in the south,
and yields of crops are also higher in the northeast. Mechanization of
most of the agricultural operations in communes, where sideline enterprises have been established, is progressing at a rapid rate because of
labour supply constraints. Mechanization will increase the labour
productivity which has been decreasing in the past, but it will be necessary to formulate a rational mechanization policy considering its impact
on yield of crops, and employment of agricultural workers.

5.   Import of grains

The "commercial grain", grain that moves within the country (also
called "commodity grain"), may be about 60 million tons, nearly 20 percent of the grain output. The "commercial grain" is vitally important
to the regime to feed China's urban population and key groups such as

military forces, to make up deficits in backward areas, calamity
stricken areas, and regions which produce industrial crops and to meet
industrial and export needs. China's net import of grain averaged 8.7
million tons [1]/ (mostly wheat) during the last three years (1977/78-79/80),
forming only about 3.0 percent of the average total grain production
(306 million tons). However, these imports are of far greater importance
to the country as they form about 15 percent of the "commercial grains".
The level of net imports planned for the medium and long-run is not only
important for China but also for other countries because of its future
impact on the world market.

6.   Investment allocation

Per capita GNP may have more than doubled in the last quarter
century. A large proportion of the increase has been reinvested as
only a portion has gone to increase consumption of all kinds and there
has been little, if any, rise in per capita consumption of food staples.

It would be useful to identify investments already made, which
have not yet started giving full returns, and to take urgent measures
for getting maximum returns from them, including making further investments required for the incomplete projects. Generally, the returns to
additional investments on incomplete projects are higher than for investments in new projects.

7.   Financing

Ninety percent of the State's revenues come from profit remittances
from State enterprises, turn-over taxes based on Industrial and Commercial Consolidated tax, and income tax on profits of collectively-owned
enterprises. Less than 10 percent comes from agricultural taxes, custom
duties, tax on slaughterhouses, salt production and urban real estate
and from sundry licensing fees on vehicles and ships. According to the
decision taken at the Third Session of the Fifth National Congress
(August-September 1980), the State-owned enterprises, instead of turning

---

1/ The forecast for net import of grain for 1980/81 is 14 million tons.

their profits over to the State, will pay profit taxes, and regulatory
and resource taxes. This change might decrease the funds available to
the State. Furthermore, the proportion of the reserve fund (mostly for
investment), in the distribution of agricultural gross output has been
decreased; it will further reduce the investment funds available within
the agricultural sector. Therefore, alternative means to secure adequate
funds for agricultural development will need to be found.

8.   Income distribution

Sideline agricultural and non-agricultural enterprises have been
established rapidly since 1977 in communes located in the vicinity of
cities and towns and in some outlying progressive communes. In some
cases, the income from these enterprises surpasses the income from agricultural pursuits, and consequently, the income of these communes has
increased substantially. Incomes, in general, of communes which do not
have such a locational advantage, have increased at a moderate rate.
Therefore, it has widened the gap in income between the communes with
and without sideline enterprises. For instance, in the Ta Li Commune
located near Canton, Guangdong province, per capita income in 1979 was
239 yuan as compared to 90 yuan in communes located in the interior.

It is very likely that the income gaps between the above-mentioned
two sets of communes will further widen, unless special policies and
programmes are undertaken to speed up the development of communes located in the interior of the country.

III. AGRICULTURAL POLICIES AND INCENTIVES

A. Agricultural policies, incentives and related institutions

The agricultural policies pursued since liberation can be grouped into four categories: land reform; collectivization-communisation; capital formation of agriculture; and alteration of terms of trade between agriculture and industry in favour of agriculture and the peasants. Land reform and collectivization have already been discussed; this section deals with agricultural prices, agricultural taxes, agricultural credit, workpoint system and some other policies related to agriculture.

1. Agricultural prices

A major objective of agricultural price policies has been to close systematically the gap between the prices received by communes for agricultural supplies and prices they pay for industrial products for agricultural inputs and consumption. In November 1953, the "Scheme of planned purchase and planned supply of foodgrain" was introduced as a pioneer to the comprehensive agricultural procurement system in China. (Foodgrains include wheat, rice, coarse grains, potatoes/sweet potatoes and soyabean.) This scheme was later extended to cover major cash crops such as cotton, oil bearing crops, sugar and livestock products. Vegetables from a commune near a city are sold to a vegetable company at fixed prices. Presently prices of most agricultural products, including vegetables and fruits, are fixed by the State or its commercial organization, and the State has thus monopolistic and monopsonistic powers in the marketing of these commodities. The system for sales to the State on a voluntary basis for the excess quantities over the purchase quota, was introduced mainly for foodgrain in 1959, and later it was applied to any product sold by the collectives to the State in excess of the original fixed purchase quota.

The two-tier purchase system, pricing for compulsory purchases – which on an average are about 25 percent of production of grains – and pricing for voluntary sales by communes to the State for the excess produce, has been the main instrument employed for providing price

incentives for increasing agricultural production and narrowing the
"scissor's difference" between prices of agricultural and industrial
products.

The purchase prices of the planned commodities have been raised
nine times since 1949, and the latest increase was in 1979 when the prices
for purchase quotas were moved upwards by 20 percent and for voluntary
sales by 50 percent. On the other hand, during this period, prices of
inputs supplied by the industry to agriculture have been reduced 6 to 10
times, amounting to a 48 percent cumulative reduction. It was officially
claimed that the prices for the planned commodities in 1975 were more
than doubled those in 1950, and consequently the agriculture terms of
trade were improved by 45 percent during 1950-75. The terms of trade
must have further improved substantially since 1975, as prices of planned
commodities have been further increased while prices of inputs have not
been increased and in some cases have even been reduced. It is estimated that the farmers gained 10 million yuan over 1978 with the increase in agricultural prices in 1979.

The purchase quotas are now fixed for a period of about 5 years.
The collectives which succeed in expanding output during this period
can sell their excess produce on a voluntary basis at a higher price.
Thus a time-lag in the reassessment of the purchase quotas encourages
the continued development of planned products.

In addition to the price premium, the collectives which exceed
the basic purchase quotas could also be awarded special ration coupons
for purchasing such essential commodities as foodgrain and chemical
fertilizers, according to the agreement reached by the commercial organs
and the collectives concerned.

There is only a slight difference in purchase prices of planned
products in different parts of the country irrespective of the transport
cost. Therefore, the transport cost is an indirect subsidy particular
to the regions from which the produce must be transported long distances
to the consumption centers.

2.   Agricultural taxes

The agricultural tax on agricultural output is assessed as a fixed amount of gross output, under normal conditions, and it is fixed for a specific period of time. Since the tax revision had not been done frequently, the agricultural tax rate declined from 12 percent of gross output in 1952 to about 5 percent in 1974, and presently it is estimated to be about 3.2 percent of gross output. The proportion of agricultural tax varies from commune to commune depending on the progress they made in agricultural development. For example, in 1979 it was 2.8 percent in the China-Japan Friendship Commune near Beijing, 1.8 percent in the suburban Long March Commune near Shanghai and 3.1 percent in Jin Ma Commune in Sichuan province.

Since tax is fixed for a certain period, no additional tax is laid on any increase in the agricultural output achieved during that period. Therefore, the tax proportion to agricultural output is reduced on account of increases in agricultural production and upward revisions in prices, if any, during that period.

There are some tax exemptions for promoting the development of new lands and economic diversifications. In 1979, the limit for tax exemption for small subsidary enterprises was increased and farmers gained about 1 million yuan from this tax reduction. Agricultural tax can be exempted for legally expanded areas from 1 to 3 years, for waste land cultivated by immigrant workers for a period of 3 to 5 years, which may be extended to 7 years for tea estates and forests developed in mountainous areas. The tax exemption is also granted for commune enterprises, the products and incomes from which are directly used for farming.

3.   Consumption subsidies

Grain and some other agricultural products are sold to consumers below their cost prices to the State, and the subsidies thus provided by the State are substantial. In some cases, the communes are encouraged to consume such commodities for which there are surpluses over the purchase quota. For example, in Chang Chiao Commune in Sichuan province,

for each pig slaughtered and consumed from the surplus, the production
team receives 3 yuan from the State as a subsidy in addition to the
fixed price (cash price plus 25 kg. of grain).

4.   Agricultural credit

The State Agricultural Bank was established in 1963 and it is
responsible for providing agricultural credit. It has its branches down
to the commune level and there are credit groups at the level of the
brigades and production teams which act as agents of the agricultural
bank. There are about 50,000 credit cooperatives at present. The following interest rates are charged for various loans to communes,
brigades and teams:

- production credit (agriculture and enterprises) for
  1 year, 4.32 percent;

- equipment and infrastructure for 1 or 2 years, 2.16 percent;

- consumption credit to individuals for 1 year, 4.32 percent;
  and

- loans for disaster and calamities for 1 year, interest free.

5.   Purchase and supply cooperatives

The Supply and Purchase Cooperatives have three major activities:
i) supplies of inputs and materials; ii) purchase of agricultural products from communes; and iii) sales of consumption goods.

In order to improve the efficiency of the operation of the Purchase and Supply Cooperatives in Sichuan province on a pilot scale,
integration of agriculture, commerce and industry is being tried and
joint enterprises of Supply and Purchase Cooperatives and communes have
been established with a dominant role granted to the communes. The commune acts as a sub-company in these joint enterprises to the county Supply and Purchase Cooperative. This arrangement ensures the supply of
required inputs and facilitates the disposal of agricultural produce.
Furthermore, about 90 percent of the profits of this sub-company remain
with the communes and only 10 percent goes to the county Supply and
Purchase Cooperative. In the past, about 80 percent of the profits used
to go to the State Supply and Purchase Cooperatives.

6.   Other incentives

    The State offers some other incentives such as: interest-free or
low-interest loans for infrastructure development and farm mechanization, and advances funds for encouraging the production of cash crops
and sidelines; subsidization of the production of agricultural machines
at the county and commune levels; granting subsidies on sales of a
number of industrial products for farm use such as diesel oil and elec-
tricity, which are 30 percent cheaper for farms than for industrial enterprises; giving priorities for supply of manufactured goods to areas that
offer more agricultural and sideline products to the States.

7.   Sideline enterprises

    The State has given many incentives, institutional as well as
material, for expanding the scope and production of sideline enterprises
in the communes. Consequently there has been significant progress in
establishing enterprises and increasing their production since 1977. The
communes, particularly with locational advantages, have ventured into a
variety of small-scale industrial enterprises in addition to agro-
industrial enterprises. In 1979, the China-Japan Friendship Commune near
Beijing established five sideline enterprises (producing toilet paper,
machine tools, veterinary medicines, needles and milk products),
and they contributed about 46 percent (including livestock) of the gross
output; the remaining 54 percent of the output came from crop and vegetable production. In the suburban Long March Commune near Shanghai, there
are 14 sideline enterprises at the commune level (manufacturing rubber,
baskets, shoes, farm tools, broadcasting and movie shows, leasing of
transport means, etc.) and the production teams' share in the gross output was 37 percent; the remaining share came from the brigades and commune enterprises. In this commune, about 400,000 yuan were distributed
from the brigades and commune enterprises to the production teams as a
reward for their collective ownership of these enterprises. The Chengdong Commune near Shanghai has six sideline enterprises (manufacturing
farm machinery, chemical fertilizers, cloth, plastic, wood articles and
electric sockets) at the commune level and 29 at the brigade level. The
industrial enterprises contributed as high as 60 percent to the gross

output of the commune and in addition 18 percent of the gross output
came from agricultural sideline enterprises; only the remaining 22 percent came from agriculture and livestock production. In Jin Ma Commune
in Sichuan province, in one brigade there are as many as 23 sideline
enterprises (fish farming, pig raising, tree nursery, oil processing,
sericulture, manufacture of furniture and cement blocks, barber, tea
and confectionery shops, etc.) and this brigade did not give any rewards
for ownership to the production team as these teams are well developed.
In Chang Chiao Commune in Sichuan province, the income from sideline
production has increased six times since 1976. In Ta Li Commune in
Guangdong province, the sideline enterprises contributed about 67 percent to the gross output.

In addition to collective sideline enterprises mentioned above,
the production pattern of private plots is being diverted to support
individual sideline enterprises, and to supply products directly to the
market. For instance, the area under fodder is being expanded to raise
livestock production, particularly pigs, and the area under vegetables
is increasing, especially to supply their produce to the markets.

Most of the products from the collective and individual sideline
enterprises can be sold on the free market.

8.   Workpoint system

"From each according to his ability, and to each according to his
work" is the fundamental job allocation and income distribution principle
in a socialistic society. Since the Revolution in 1949, China has used
mainly piece-rate and time-rate systems for work assessment at different
stages of its socialistic transformation. Many variations of these two
methods have been adopted by the communes. But the general principles
of these two methods are as follows:

Piece-rate system - All farm tasks are classified into various
categories which are in turn allocated to groups of members with the
agreed norms and number of workpoints. The evaluation of the work performance is then conducted by members and the collective management

according to the agreed norms. This is the basis of awarding the work-points to various working groups and their associated individual members.

The popular application of the piece-rate system in the people's communes began in 1962 after the launching of the "Sixty Regulations" which proposed to production teams the following two principles:

(i) "Regulation No. 31: For the purpose of organizing pro-duction, production team management may divide its labour force into permanent or temporary working groups that will be responsible for the particular works assigned by the management on a seasonal or annual basis. A strict system of production responsibility should be established and pro-duction responsibility should be assigned down to the working groups or the individuals;

(ii) "Regulation No. 32: In view of realising the principle of 'to each according to his/her work' and of avoiding egalitarianism, production team management should gradually set up the norms and rates of payment for various farm works, and adopt the method of norm management. This should apply to all works that could be undertaken on such basis. 'Cal-culating workpoints on the basis of work done' can be intro-duced to farm work which is not suitable for using the method of norm management. The norms and rates of payments of various tasks should be assessed in terms of the time and technical requirements for fulfilling the tasks by the average member. More technical tasks and heavier works should be given more workpoints, and the quality of these tasks should be clearly stated." 1/

Under this system, most tasks are allocated to a group consisting of a few individuals and some tasks which are not feasible for group per-formance are given to individuals.

Time-rate system - In the time-rate method of basic workpoints with flexible assessment, "a basic number of workpoints is fixed for each member after his working capability and skill are appraised, and the specific number of workpoints he earns each day is a modification of this basic number through assessment of his actual performance that day by

---

1/ A Revised Draft on the Working Regulations for Rural People's Communes (referred to as Sixty Regulations), Peking, People's Publishing House, 1962.

fellow members, with an increase in case of good performance and a deduction in case of poor" [1]. Flexible assessment is designed to check the quality of work done by each individual worker.

Members of a production team adopting this method are classified into various categories, considering their physical conditions and skills. There is no general rule for determining the number of categories and allotting workpoints to each category of workers. In this method egalitarianism is emphasised by keeping the difference in workpoints allocated to the various category of workers on the time basis as small as possible. A high level of socialistic consciousness among the members is thus a basic prerequisite to conterbalance the impediment to individual incentives in the method.

In short, the piece-rate system stresses the principle "to each according to his work" and provides incentives for better performance while the time-rate system emphasises egalitarianism by relying on the responsibility of the members to contribute their work which is not only guided by their personal gains but also is inspired by their consciousness to further economic and social development.

During the initial years of cooperative movement the piece-rate payment system was extensively used for work assessment among elementary agricultural producers' cooperatives and this system continued in the advanced agricultural producers' cooperatives in which the "rental income" was abolished. A radical change in the method of work assessment and income distribution took place soon after the setting up of the commune system in 1958 in which egalitarianism was stressed, consequently the piece-rate payment system was very much de-emphasised and the time-rate method was encouraged, particularly during the "Great Leap Forward". The promotion of the time-rate system must have aggravated further the damage done to agriculture by national calamities during 1959-61. In 1962 "a revised draft on the Working Conditions for Rural People's Communes" was formulated and egalitarianism was severely criticised and a

---

[1] Model regulations for an agricultural producers' cooperative, Peking Foreign Language Press, 1976.

piece-rate system called "norm management and workpoint calculations based on work done" was recommended. During the Cultural Revolution, the time-rate system was put into command, the principles of "Sixty Regulations" were challenged and the piece-rate system was denounced and "to each according to his work" was criticised as a bourgeois instrument that led to greater income inequality and a possible emergence of a new bourgeois in a socialistic society. Since 1976, the "Sixty Regulations" have again become the basic guidelines for collective management. It is estimated that presently about 70-80 percent of the production teams are using the piece-rate method to varying degrees. For example, in the Long March Commune near Shanghai, the piece-rate method is used for assessment of 50 percent of the total work and time rate is used for the remaining 50 percent.

Output based method: A new method linking the reward for work with output and cost effectiveness in order to provide collective as well as individual incentives for increasing production and income is being experimented in some communes. For instance, in Cheng Chiao Commune in Sichuan province, a production team consisting of 50 workers has been divided into three groups. Each group has been given specific area and its production plan, and no change has been made in the area allotted to them during the last two years. All three groups over-fulfilled their production and purchase quotas and they received 60 percent of the surplus production as their income in addition to their share from the planned output.

There are many variations for this experiment to link reward for work with output as against the piece-rate in which reward was related to the specific job done, and in the time-rate to the time put in perform the specific work.

A simple example for relating work reward to output follows:

	Group A	Group B	Group C	Total
Area	same	same	same	
Number of workers	same	same	same	
Number of households	same	same	same	
Output planned (yuan)	700	700	700	2100
Cost and collective share (yuan)	200	200	200	600
Individual share (yuan)	500	500	500	1500
Workpoints required-planned (number)	200	200	200	600
Individual share/workpoints (yuan)	2.5	2.5	2.5	2.5
Actual output achieved (yuan)	850	800	700	2350
Cost and collective share (yuan)	200	200	200	600
Actual individual share (yuan)	650	600	500	1750
Actual individual share/planned workpoints (yuan)	3.7	3.0	2.5	2.92
Workpoints actually used (number)	220	210	200	630
Actual individual share/actual workpoints (yuan)	2.96	2.90	2.50	2.78
Distribution of planned individual share (yuan)	500	500	500	1500
Surplus over planned individual share (yuan)	150	100	–	250
Distribution of surplus (yuan)	100	90	60	250
Total income of group (yuan)	600	590	560	1750
Total income of group/actual workpoints (yuan)	2.73	2.81	2.80	2.78

The distribution of surplus over the planned output is divided among the groups according to a procedure agreed on at the formulation of the production plan. A major consideration in formulating this procedure is to keep the income differentials within reasonable limits. It may therefore be seen from the example that a group doesn't get the benefit of all the excess production, as part of it is distributed to the groups which have produced less surplus. However, if a group doesn't meet the planned output, it is likely to be punished by the penalties agreed upon at the formulation of the production plan. For example, in Cheng Chiao Commune it was decided in 1978/79 to deduct six workpoints from a group for each 50 kg. of underfulfillment of the planned output for grains, but all the group surpassed the planned output with varying amounts in that year. Also it is not necessary that all the surplus output is distributed; a part may be retained as a reserve fund.

The groups have flexibility to use more purchased inputs, such as fertilizers and pesticides, than their planned levels. But they have to bear expenses for such additional inputs as these expenses will not be deducted from the gross output as a cost to arrive at the individual share for distribution to groups. However, as shown in the above example, a group can use more labour and improve management to increase production and income.

In this method, the workpoints, besides providing the usual basic criterion for distribution of income, are also used for comparing labour productivity and management efficiency among the groups and for determining guidelines for improvements for the groups with comparatively low labour and management efficiency. For example, the value of actual individual share / actual workpoints clearly show in the illustration that returns to per unit workpoint and management are highest in group A and lowest in group C.

This system is at present in an experimental stage and it offers opportunities to include in it in the future a number of factors for improving management and increasing labour and management efficiency and income, e.g. more freedom to groups in formulation of production plans, determination and reduction of costs, purchase of inputs, processing and marketing of produce, etc.

In the sideline enterprises, the time-rate and piece-rate systems also are generally used for assessing the work of members of the commune, but in some cases they are paid wages and salaries. For instance, in the Ta Li Commune, due to shortage of labour in the commune, workers from outside the commune are employed in the sideline enterprises and these workers are paid wages and salaries. Similarly, the members of this commune working in the commune sideline enterprises are also paid wages and salaries, but they have to pay 10 percent of their wages and salaries to their respective production teams. As the incomes of persons working in the sideline enterprises are generally higher than those in the production teams, this measure is directed at keeping a certain level of income parity between the commune members working in production teams and those working in the sideline enterprises. However, in this commune at the brigade level, the returns to workers in the sideline enterprises are determined according to their workpoints, and these returns are paid to the respective production teams from where they get their share. Thus a variety of methods suitable to local conditions are being employed for employment of workers and distribution of income in the sideline enterprises.

B. Major issues concerning agricultural policies and incentives
1. Production pattern adjustments

The cultivated area in China is restricted and intensification of land use is comparatively high. Therefore, there is not much "leeway" for increasing area under a crop unless the area under another crop is decreased. Thus, the adjustments in the cropping pattern will most probably be accomplished by substituting one crop for another, particularly in the medium run.

Great emphasis was given to enhancing grain output in the past through price policies, institutional and political measures, and the grain crops replaced substantially the area under other crops. Now that more flexibility is allowed in formulating cropping patterns and over-emphasis on the grain production has been eliminated, it is very likely that the area under foodgrains will decrease in the medium term, and consequently their output growth rate may decline or even their production may fall unless strong measures are taken to increase grain yields, such as increased use of crucial inputs like fertilizers, pesticides and irrigation. However, the adjustments in production patterns are expected to contribute towards achieving higher overall agricultural growth rate.

The country's imports of foodgrains averaged about 9 million tons during the last three years. The reduction in grain production will further increase the grain imports, which will have important national and international implications.

2. Price adjustments

Strong measures were taken in the past to raise the level of agricultural prices vis-à-vis those of industrial products, particularly the agricultural inputs supplied by industry. Thus the terms of trade in

favour of agriculture have been considerably improved. These price
adjustments have so far been based on historical experience. How long
such adjustments in terms of trade should continue and to what magnitude,
are some of the important aspects which require thorough investigation.

3.   Allocative efficiency of resources

Priority is given for supply of manufactured goods and agricultural inputs to areas that offer more agricultural and sideline products
to the State. It may lead to malallocation of agricultural inputs
which are in short supply. For instance, the progressive communes receive comparatively large quantities of fertilizers per unit of area as
compared to the relatively less developed communes, and they tend to use
the fertilizers to the level at which marginal cost of using the fertilizer is equal to marginal revenue from the produce. However, in the
relatively less developed communes the use of fertilizer is well below
the optimum doses, though in their case the marginal returns to use of
additional fertilizer are likely to be higher than at the progressive
communes, assuming similar shape of the production functions. Therefore,
the present system of distribution of fertilizers may lead to less than
optimum returns.

4.   Subsidies

The amount of subsidies provided for the purchase of agricultural
products by the State and its commercial organizations is increasing with
the growth in production and increase in purchase quotas, and by
periodically raising the rate of the subsidies. Similarly, consumption
subsidies are also growing with increase in consumption. These production
and consumption subsidies put a considerable strain on the budgetary resources of the State. It will, therefore, be useful to conduct studies
on gradual reduction of these subsidies through appropriate measures such
as allocation of investments, adjustments in cropping patterns, etc.

5.   Investment funds

In the past, substantial investment resources in the agricultural
sector were generated by restricting private consumption. The expansion
of sideline enterprises and relaxation of restrictions on the free market

will lead to expansion of opportunities of, and temptation for, increasing private consumption. What incentives should be provided and which measures should be undertaken to continue to raise the required amount of investment funds in the rural areas in order to keep a proper balance between consumption, savings and investment, should be important matters for the State and the provincial governments.

6.   Role of markets

A socialistic economy generally follows the economic law that the value of a commodity is determined by the amount of socially necessary labour spent on its production, and that the commodities are exchanged at equal values. The above law of value and market mechanism are generally regarded as incompatible. Therefore, as the role of central planning is enlarged, that of the market is diminished. In a dominant central planning system, if an effective mechanism for determining the needs of the society for commodities is lacking, inconsistencies between supply and demand occur, causing gluts of certain goods and scarcity of some others. It further leads to distortion of prices and imbalances in the development of various sectors. Considering the need for proper balance among the interests of the State, the collective and the individual in planning, China has recently relaxed a number of constraints on the free market. Important measures taken in this direction are that the surplus over the purchase quotas of the commodities controlled by the State and its commercial organizations, and most of the products from the individual and collective sideline enterprises, can now be sold in the free market.

Previously, the free market was mainly restricted to village trade fairs for sale of handicraft and some produce from private plots. Now that the role of the free market has been expanded, two important aspects need to be given serious thought:

(i)   to establish conceptual and theoretical framework to ascertain the role of market mechanism in the socialistic economy, and to carry out investigations and studies for evolving a suitable combination of market mechanism and socialistic planning for regulating the socialistic economy to attain its primary objectives; and

(ii) to strengthen the free marketing system in respect of transportation, market structures, information, quality control, etc., to provide sufficient and efficient marketing services.

7.   Manpower utilization

Incomes as well as working conditions in the collective sideline enterprises, particularly industry, are generally better than those in the production teams engaged in agricultural activities. There is, thus, a tendency for managers, technicians and good workers to move from the production teams to these sideline enterprises. Though it is an appropriate adjustment for improving the utilization of manpower resources, it may seriously curtail the technical and managerial resources available to primary agricultural activities, and affect the performance of these activities adversely. Therefore, there is a need to systematically upgrade the technical and managerial capabilities of manpower in the agricultural sector.

8.   Income inequalities

Incentives provided through prices and tax policies, concessions for establishment of sideline enterprises, preferences given to progressive communes for supply of agricultural inputs, access to free markets, etc., tend to increase individual incomes faster at progressive communes and communes with locational advantages, than in comparatively less efficient communes, and communes in the interior of the Country. Therefore, income inequalities among regions and among communes within a region will widen unless appropriate economic and fiscal measures are taken to develop the lagging-behind regions and less efficient communes within regions. A beginning has already been made by implementing various measures, for example, granting of interest-free loans to develop sideline enterprises in the communes located in the interior of the country.

Within a commune, incomes of the members engaged in collective sideline enterprises are generally higher than those working in production teams. Though some measures are already being implemented to keep a certain level of income parity between the above-mentioned two groups, this aspect should be more thoroughly investigated, particularly in view of the rapidly expanding sideline enterprises, in order to keep this disparity within reasonable limits.

IV. AGRICULTURAL EDUCATION, TRAINING AND RESEARCH

A. Existing structure

Amongst the more serious dislocations of the turbulent years 1966-76, was the breakdown in agricultural education, training and research. The universities/institutions were closed and staff sent to work elsewhere. The research institutions suffered a similar fate and much valuable data was lost. The training programme was allowed to disintegrate. There has been an orderly resumption of activities since 1976 and the inherent system has the merit to permit recovery but it will take some time to rectify the damage done.

Formal agricultural education is offered at two levels:
— at degree and post-graduate level by agricultural universities and institutes of agriculture which also have university status; and
— at senior secondary school level by agricultural secondary schools.

There are 45 agricultural universities or institutes of agriculture of equal status, two of which were newly opened recently. Every province or municipality now has at least one such institution - Sichuan province has four. The teaching staff is 24,000 with 900 at senior levels, 5,000 up to the grade of lecturer and the rest as teaching assistants and below. The student body is 45,000, although the number of post-graduate students is rather modest at 445.

The regular teaching programme is of four years' duration, divided into eight semesters; three year specialised programmes are also offered. Unified entrance examinations are administered by the State and the assignment of graduates for employment is also a State responsibility. Post-graduates are mainly assigned to do research and graduates assigned to production work.

There are seven institutions of higher agricultural education administered by the Ministry of Agriculture in conjunction with the Ministry of Education. They are:

- Beijing Agricultural University at Beijing
- Nanking Institute of Agriculture at Nanking
- South China Institute of Agriculture at Guangzhou
- Central China Institute of Agriculture at Wuhan
- South-west Institute of Agriculture at Chongqing
- Institute of Agriculture for North-West China near Xi'an
- North-east Institute of Agriculture at Shenyang.

The other 38 institutions are supervised by the agricultural and education departments of the provincial governments although there is a close tie-up with the Bureau of Agricultural Education of the Ministry of Agriculture. The seven central institutions are generally better staffed than the provincial institutions.

There are 210 agricultural secondary schools with a total enrolment of about 80,000 students and with 8,500 teachers. In the past 30 years 540,000 students have graduated. The teaching programme is of two years' duration concentrating on agricultural subjects since the students have already graduated from general secondary schools.

In-service training of leading cadres is undertaken at various levels. The seven central agricultural universities/institutes run four-month general agriculture courses for senior staff at provincial, prefecture and county levels. Similarly, the agricultural bureaux at provincial/prefecture level are responsible for in-service training of cadres at sub-county level. Such courses are usually run at agricultural secondary schools or at agricultural cadres training centres. There is also a spare-time education programme which provides correspondence courses for staff and youth in rural areas.

Research is organised through the Chinese Academy of Agricultural Science as the apex body. There are also well established national institutes in selected disciplines and all the agricultural universities/institutes are brought into the network, each specializing in selected fields. There is also a network of Provincial Research Institutions going down to the county level. Some communes have small research stations attached to them where field demonstrations are carried out. The County

Research Stations train the commune research station staff and also send their experts to help at the commune level. The Agricultural Colleges also send their experts to the nearby communes to carry out field work and have established close working arrangements with the provincial and county research stations to prevent overlapping. Each brigade has experts in machinery, irrigation, and selected crops, who serve all production teams. The teams themselves have technicians in selected fields such as plant protection, cultivation, water and seed. These technicians are selected from amongst the team members themselves and receive training at the commune research station or at county level where appropriate.

With modernization as its goal in the agricultural sector, the People's Republic of China lays great stress on the improvement of agricultural education and training to bring modern agricultural methods to the assistance of the state farms, the communes and the production brigades and teams. The Fourth Session of the Central Committee of the 11th Congress of the Communist Party of China, held on 28 September 1979, passed a resolution calling for: the improvement and perfection of the key agricultural universities and colleges; the training of a large number of experts and management personnel in modern agricultural science and technology, and the construction of an integrated and well coordinated agricultural scientific research system and an agricultural extension network. In the first instance, an FAO/UNDP project entitled "Strengthening Agricultural Education" has been formulated by a four-man mission fielded by NSHE 1/. The preliminary phase of two years' duration, starting in September 1980, assists five key agricultural universities and colleges to enhance the competence of its professional staff and augment the physical facilities with the aim of upgrading and expanding the training of teaching staff, researchers, administrators and extension workers serving the university. The preliminary phase will cost US $ 8000,000 as UNDP's contribution and 4.4 million yuan as the Chinese contribution. Further assistance is expected in a second phase starting

---

1/ Details of the proposal can be found in the report of the Mission (Report of the FAO Project Formulation Mission, 6 May to 14 June 1980) and in Project Document CPR/80/003 "Strengthening Agricultural Education in China", and are therefore not included here.

38

in 1982. In addition, bilateral donors, particularly the USA, have expressed interest in assisting Chinese Agricultural Universities.

B.   Major issues
1.   Agricultural education

Fortunately, the agricultural education system previously established in China can meet the needs provided it is suitably strengthened on the lines suggested by the FAO mission. This means that middle-level teaching staff have to be trained in modern methods and the older staff permitted access to refresher courses to bring them up-to-date with the latest scientific discoveries and techniques. The second phase of the FAO/UNDP project will require a substantially larger input to have any significant impact. There is also a need for simultaneous bilateral programmes on similar lines.

2.   Training

The training system for cadres at the national universities/institutions and at the provincial level has to be re-introduced. Since, in the turbulent years, great prominence was given to manual work rather than scientific knowledge, most of the cadres are unskilled in the latest techniques.

3.   Research

Although the system exists, there is much to be done to revitalize it. Some of the commune research stations which we saw were in poor condition and the staff inadequately trained. Now that the situation has changed and modernization is the goal, there is great scope to strengthen the whole research and training structure with coordinated research trials, integrated training programmes, etc. on the lines adopted in most developed countries, notably the USA, and in some developing countries (ICAR in India, PICAR in the Philippines). FAO's research and training personnel can assist substantially in this area.

MAIN LOCATIONS VISITED AND PRINCIPAL OFFICIALS
AND PEOPLE MET

28.7.80   Arrival in Beijing.

           Reception and Dinner.

29.7.80   Discussions.

30.7.80   Sightseeing.

People met in Beijing from 28 - 30.7.80:

Hao Zhongsi	Vice Minister, Ministry of Agriculture
Wu Daxing	Senior Agro-Economist, Institute of Agri-Economics, Academy of Agro-Sciences
Ma Ling	Deputy Director, Bureau of Foreign Affairs, Ministry of Agriculture
Zhang Shizhan	Division Chief, International Division, Bureau of Foreign Affairs, Ministry of Agriculture
Fan Yao Hui	Deputy Division Chief, Bureau of Planning, Ministry of Agriculture
Cui Zheng Dong	Division Chief, Bureau of People's Communes, Ministry of Agriculture
Cai Xinyi	Division Chief, Ministry of Land Reclamation and State Farms
Hao	Engineer, Ministry of Agro-Machines
Huang Xiaheng	Division Chief, Ministry of Water Conservancy
* Wu Tian-Xi	Deputy Chief Engineer, Ministry of Agriculture
* Zhang Jiankai	Interpreter

* Accompanied the Mission throughout their visit.

31.7.80   Visit to China-Japan Friendship Commune, outside Beijing.

          Huang Jinzhong   Vice-Dean of Commune Office

          Other staff members

1.8.80   Travel to Shanghai. Reception.
Discussions.

          Shi Zhi Lu   Deputy Director, Bureau of
                                 Agriculture

          Yang Yuchen   Deputy Director, Foreign Affairs
                                 Division

          Jiang Zhong Tang   Staff, Foreign Affairs Division

       Visit to Chang Zhen (Long March) Commune.

          Shen Huongqi   Vice-Chairman of Commune

2.8.80   Visit to Chengdong Commune, Jiating County, 73 km. north of
Shanghai.

          Lu Jianxin   Deputy Governor, Jiating County

          Li Chengxun   Vice-Dean, Office of Foreign
                                 Affairs, Jiating County

          Chen Zhilong   Vice-Chairman, Chengdong Commune

3.8.80   Visit to exhibit of industrial goods. Sightseeing.

4.8.80   Travel to Xi'an, Shaanxi Province. Briefing and discussions

          Xu Ruzhou   Division Chief, Division of
                                 Science and Technology, Bureau
                                 of Agriculture, Xi'an

          Liu Suicang   Staff, Bureau of Agriculture,
                                 Xi'an

5.8.80   Visit to North-Western College of Agriculture, Wugong County,
Shaanxi Province.

          Xu Xuan   Vice-President, College

          Wan Jianzhong   Vice Dean of Economic Department,
                                 Agro-Economic Professor

Ma Hongyun	Professor, Dean of Economic Department
Huang Shengquan	Professor
Wang Guangsen	Professor, Agro-Economy
Li	Director, Institute of Agro-Economics, Shaanxi Academy of Agro-Forestry Sciences

6.8.80   Sightseeing. Departure for Chengdu, by train.

7.8.80   Arrival in <u>Chengdu</u>, Sichuan Province.

Briefing.

Yang Zhong	Deputy Governor of Sichuan Province
Suai Ren	Deputy Director, Bureau of Agriculture, Sichuan Province
Lo Suhua	Division Chief, Commune Division, Bureau of Agriculture

Visit to Jin Ma (Golden Horse) Commune, 30 km. from Chengdu

Hu Guilian (Mrs.)	Chairman, Commune
Fu Shaoyun	Leader of Brigade
Yiu	Director, Office of Foreign Affairs Prefecture
Liang	Staff, Office of Foreign Affairs, District

Dinner at Commune and further discussions.

8.8.80   Visit to Cheng Chiao Commune, Kwanghan County, Sichuan Province.

Zhang Zhiquen (Mrs.)	Vice Governor, Kwanghan County
Li Ming Ying	Chairman, Commune
Pi Yunsu	Dean, Office of Agriculture, Guanghan County

Cai Shilun	Manager, Joint Enterprises of Agriculture, Industry, Commerce, Cheng Chiao Commune
Yu Zili	Leader of Production Team

Evening reception and dinner given by Deputy Governor of Sichuan Province.

9.8.80 Discussions.

Tang Hongqian	Deputy Director, Research Institute of Agro-Economics, Sichuan Province
Ni Guigen	Division Chief, Bureau of Communes and Brigade Enterprises
Cai Jingzhong	Division Chief, Bureau of Planning and Finance

Visit to Dujiangyan Irrigation System (Chengdu). Sightseeing.

10.8.80 Travel to Guangzhou, Guangdong Province.

Briefing and sightseeing.

Zhou Jianfu	Deputy Director, Bureau of Agriculture, Guangdong Province
Han Hung Guang	Staff, Bureau of Agriculture, Guangzhou

11.8.80 Visit to Ta-Li Commune, 20 km. from Guangzhou, Guangdong Province.

Lin Wuxung	Deputy Chairman, Ta-Li Commune, Nanhai County

Dinner given by Dr. Islam.

12.8.80 Departure from China.

BIBLIOGRAPHY

Aziz, Sartaj: Rural Development: Learning from China. Macmillan Press Ltd., London, 1978, 201 pp.

Barker, Randolph and Sinha, Radha (eds.): Cornell Workshop on Agricultural and Rural Development in the People's Republic of China (Rep (Report), Cornell International Agriculture Mimeograph 74. Cornell University, Ithaca, N.Y., October 1979.

Barnett, A. Doak: China and World Food Problems. Brookings, Washington, D.C., March 1978.

Beijing Review article: "Inquiry Into Guidelines for Agriculture", Beijing Review, No. 4, pp. 20-26, January 28, 1980.

Beijing Review article: "The Agricultural Development Programme", Beijing Review, No. 12, pp. 14-20, March 24, 1980.

Berger, Roland: "Economic Planning in China", China's Road to Development, Maxwell, Neville (ed.), 2nd ed., pp. 169-203. Pergamon Press, Oxford, 1979.

China Business Review article: "China's New Economic Priorities", China Business Review, pp. 36-39, July-August 1979.

China, People's Rep. of: "Sixty Regulations", A Revised Draft on the Working Regulations for Rural People's Communes. People's Publishing House, Peking, 1962.

China, People's Rep. of: Model Regulations for An Agricultural Producer's Co-operative. Foreign Language Press, Peking, 1976.

Current Scene article: "China's 10-Year Programme for the Development of Agriculture and the National Economy (1976-1985)", Current Scene, Vol. XVI, Nos. 4 & 5, pp. 25-29, April-May 1978.

FAO: "Agricultural Development in China", State of Food and Agriculture 1978, pp. 2-27 - 2-36. FAO, Rome.

FAO: "Fulfilment of China's 1979 Economic Plan", Summary of World Broadcasts, Second Series N. 6410, May 2, 1980. FAO Statistics Division Release on Economic Information on Centrally Planned Economies, No. 28, May 7, 1980.

FAO Study Mission: Learning from China - A Report on Agriculture and the Chinese People's Communes. Regional Office for Asia and the Far East, Bangkok, 1977.

FAO/UNDP Study Tour: China: the agricultural training system. FAO Economic and Social Development Paper 11, Rome, 1980.

Guoguang, Liu and Renwei, Zhao: "Socialist Economic Planning and the
    Market", Beijing Review, No. 31, pp. 8-12, August 31, 1979.

Gurley, John G.: "Rural Development in China 1949-75, and the Lessons
    to be Learned from it", China's Road to Development, Maxwell, Neville
    (ed.), 2nd ed., pp. 5-25. Pergamon Press, Oxford, 1979.

Hua, Guofeng: "Report on the Work of the Government", Beijing Review,
    No. 27, pp. 5-21, July 6, 1979.

Khan, Azizur R.: "The Distribution of Income in Rural China", Poverty
    and Landlessness in Rural Asia, pp. 253-280. ILO, Geneva, 1977.

Khan, Azizur R.: "Taxation, Procurement and Collective Incentives in
    Chinese Agriculture", World Development, Vol. 6, pp. 827-836. Per-
    gamon Press, Oxford, 1978.

Kraus Bochum, Willy: "Peking Raises the Statistical Veil", Intereconomics,
    pp. 248-253, September/October 1979.

Lardy, Nicholas R.: "The Prospects for Chinese Agricultural Growth". A
    paper prepared for the Workshop on Agricultural and Rural Develop-
    ment in the People's Republic of China, Cornell University, Ithaca,
    N.Y., May 17-19, 1979.

London, Miriam: "Hunger in China: The Failure of a System?". A paper
    prepared for the Workshop on Agricultural and Rural Development in
    the People's Republic of China, Cornell University, Ithaca, N.Y.,
    May 17-19, 1979.

Maxwell, Neville (ed.): China's Road to Development, 2nd ed. Pergamon
    Press, Oxford, 1979, 365 pp.

Ng, Gek-boo: "Incentive policy in Chinese collective agriculture", Food
    Policy, pp. 75-86, May 1979.

Ng, Gek-boo: "Operation and Control of Individual Economic Activities in
    Collective Agriculture: The Case of China", World Employment Program-
    me Research working paper. ILO, Geneva, 1978.

Ng, Gek-boo: "Grass-root Management in Rural China: The Workpoint System
    of the People's Communes", World Employment Programme Research work-
    ing paper. ILO, Geneva, 1979.

O'Leary, Greg: "China Comes Home: The Re-integration of China into the
    World Economy", Journal of Contemporary Asia, Vol. 9, No. 4, pp. 455-
    477, 1979.

Robinson, Joan: Economic Management in China, 3rd ed. Anglo-Chinese Edu-
    cational Institute, London, 1976, 39 pp.

Robinson, Joan: Reports from China: 1953-1976. Anglo-Chinese Educational
    Institute, London, 1977.

Rawski, Thomas G.: "Chinese Economic Planning", Current Scene, Vol. XIV, No. 4, pp. 1-15, April 1976.

Sigurdson, Jon: "Rural Industrialization in China: Approaches and Results", World Development, Vol. 3, Nos. 7 & 8, pp. 526-538, July-August 1975.

State Statistical Bureau: "Communique on Fulfilment of China's 1978 National Economic Plan", Beijing Review, No. 21, pp. 37-41, July 6, 1979.

Stavis, Benedict: Making Green Revolution - The Politics of Agricultural Development in China. Cornell University, Ithaca, 1974, 287 pp.

Stavis, Benedict: The Impact of Agricultural Collectivization on Productivity in China. Center for International Studies, Cornell University, September 1977.

Stavis, Benedict: "China and the Comparative Analysis of Land Reform", Modern China, pp. 63-78, January 1978.

Stavis, Benedict: "Turning Point in China's Agricultural Policy". A paper prepared for the Workshop on Agricultural and Rural Development in the People's Republic of China, Cornell University, Ithaca, N. Y., May 17-19, 1979.

Tang, Anthony M. and Stone, Bruce: Food Production in the People's Republic of China, Research Report 15. International Food Policy Research Institute, Washington, D. C., May 1980, 177 pp.

Timmer, C. Peter and Falcon, Walter P.: "Solving China's Food Problem". A paper prepared for the Workshop on Agricultural and Rural Development in the People's Republic of China, Cornell University, Ithaca, N. Y., May 17-19, 1979.

U.S. Congress, Joint Economic Committee: China: A Reassessment of the Economy. U.S. Government Printing Office, Washington, D. C., 1975, 737 pp. (a compendium of papers).

U.S. Congress, Joint Economic Committee: Chinese Economy Post-Mao. U.S. Government Printing Office, Washington, D.C., 1978, 880 pp. (a compendium of papers).

U.S. Department of Agriculture: China: Agricultural Situation. USDA, Washington, D.C., September/October 1979, 16 pp.

Wiens, Thomas B.: "Agriculture in the Four Modernizations". A paper prepared for the Workshop on Agricultural and Rural Development in the People's Republic of China, Cornell University, Ithaca, N.Y., May 17-19, 1979.

Yu, Qiuli: "Arrangements for the 1979 National Economic Plan", Beijing Review, No. 29, pp. 7-16, July 20, 1979.